MW00641369

FRANK LLOYD WRIGHT

ON ARCHITECTURE, NATURE, AND THE HUMAN SPIRIT
A COLLECTION OF QUOTATIONS

EDITED BY
BRUCE BROOKS PFEIFFER

FRANK
LLOYD
WRIGHT ®
COLLECTION

Pomegranate
SAN FRANCISCO

Published by Pomegranate Communications, Inc.
19018 NE Portal Way, Portland OR 97230
800 227 1428 | www.pomegranate.com

Pomegranate Europe Ltd.
Unit 1, Heathcote Business Centre, Hurlbutt Road
Warwick, Warwickshire CV34 6TD, UK
[+44] 0 1926 430111 | sales@pomeurope.co.uk

Library of Congress Cataloging-in-Publication Data

Wright, Frank Lloyd, 1867–1959.
  Frank Lloyd Wright on architecture, nature, and the human spirit :
a collection of quotations / edited by Bruce Brooks Pfeiffer.
    p. cm.
  Includes bibliographical references.
  ISBN 978-0-7649-5956-1 (hardcover)
  1. Wright, Frank Lloyd, 1867–1959—Quotations. I. Pfeiffer, Bruce Brooks. II. Title.

  NA737.W7A35 2011
  720.92—dc22

                              2011009647

Pomegranate Catalog No. A198
Designed by Stephanie Odeh

Printed in China

23 22 21 20 19 18 17 16 15 14   12 11 10 9 8 7 6 5 4 3

CONTENTS

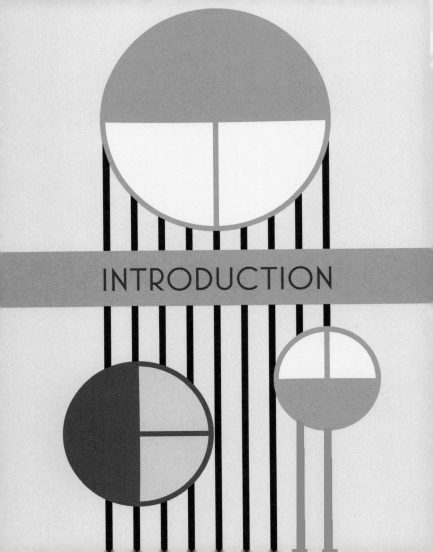

INTRODUCTION

FRANK LLOYD WRIGHT was unquestionably the most prominent, revered, and gifted architect of his time—if not, arguably, of all time. He is well known for buildings in the United States as well as in Japan, and his reputation has been reinforced by the hundreds of unbuilt designs that can be seen and studied in the many books about his work published worldwide. He not only produced great architecture in all categories, from the smallest home to a civic center of sizable proportions, he also wrote and spoke copiously about the art and craft of architecture, the fine arts, urbanism, and society. Among his most important writings are an autobiography and the many lectures he delivered in the United States and in England. His thoughts on the nature of materials, published in *The Architectural Record* in 1927 and 1928, were an early contribution to this genre. The book *A Testament,* which appeared in 1957, was part autobiography, part philosophy, and part architectural treatise.

Wright called his architecture "organic," an approach he defined in several different ways during his lifetime—it proceeded from within outward; each part was to the other parts as the whole was to its constituents; it was of its time; it was of its place; and it was meant to provide an environment of beauty for the life of mankind.

His books and public lectures were devoted to these concepts, and for him architecture was always the frame for life. "Architecture must now construct anew the whole social pattern of our time as a new order of the human spirit."[1]

He also defined his chosen art form as "that great living creative spirit which from generation to generation, from age to age, proceeds, persists, creates, according to the nature of man, and his circumstances as they both *change*."[2]

"The architect," wrote Wright on another occasion, "must be the master in the interior sense, not only of his tools, not only of his materials, but also of the human spirit. The soul of humanity is in his charge, really."[3]

And, nearly as grandly, "Man takes a positive hand in creation whenever he puts a building upon the earth beneath the sun. If he has any birthright at all, it must consist in this, that he, too, is no less a feature of the landscape than the rocks, trees, bears or bees of that nature to which he owes his being."[4]

His interests and deep concerns went beyond architecture to embrace the realms of ethics, existence, and all aspects of human behavior. In this sense, he was truly the proverbial Renaissance man. His thoughts on all these topics can be found in the writings ostensibly devoted to architecture. There is, however, another category of his writings that is far more personal—the Sunday morning talks to the apprentices who made up the Taliesin Fellowship.

The talks were a tradition at Taliesin, Wright's home and studio in southwestern Wisconsin, as well as at Taliesin West, his winter compound in Arizona. Wright and his wife Olgivanna would join the members of the fellowship for Sunday morning breakfast, and at the conclusion of the meal the room would grow quiet as all waited for Wright to speak. "Quiet seems to be descending upon the house," said Wright on one of these occasions. "When quiet descends, I suppose it's an invitation for somebody to speak, and I'm afraid that somebody is me."[5] "You know, I am getting into the position of a preacher. My father was a preacher and I remember going with my mother to church every Sunday morning and sitting down below and seeing him up in the pulpit, and here I am getting dangerously near to the similar circumstances. I don't propose to be a preacher, just as you know I don't propose to be a teacher either—except by example."[6]

Another tradition at Taliesin was the Saturday evening dinner followed by a film, booked specially for the occasion and shown in the Taliesin Playhouse with its 35mm projectors. These films came from all the major Hollywood studios, and also from France, Czechoslovakia, Italy, and Russia. Frequently a Sunday morning talk began with a review of the film shown the night before. The day after *Prelude to Fame* was shown, Wright remarked, "It is refreshing to see a movie that has in it not only something of an idea, but human sympathies and justice working out. It was charming to see that everybody in that film last night got what was coming to him."[7]

Despite his reluctance to be either a preacher or a teacher, Wright's Sunday morning talks were definitely in the nature of sermons, and regardless of his protestations, the architect was certainly imparting wisdom and serious advice. Both he and Olgivanna felt a profound sense of responsibility toward the young men and women of the fellowship, an extended family in which the Wrights acted as parents.

To assemble the current book, I combed through Wright's published writings. The other important source was those Sunday morning talks. Soon after I joined the Taliesin Fellowship in the winter of 1949, I began to regret that Wright's words shared with the fellows, which left a deep impression on me, were being lost. Even though the talks were impromptu, they struck me as too valuable to perish. Accordingly, I acquired a tape recorder and began recording. Over the next ten years, we upgraded tape recorders several times to assure the highest quality of recording possible. During that remarkable decade, we amassed approximately 250 hours of Frank Lloyd Wright on tape. Eventually we made tape-to-tape copies, which are available for study and research today. Transcripts of the tapes provided many of the quotations in the pages that follow—and in this Introduction.

Wright once confessed: "I had to choose early in my life between an honest arrogance and a hypocritical humility and I deliberately chose an honest arrogance."[8] But he qualified that statement later, saying: "I have talked of honest arrogance, but there is no such thing as honest arrogance. Arrogance is only arrogance when it has nothing under it, when it has nothing to stand on, when it is a pretense, a quackery, or a fake. When it is genuine, it is a pride that is the highest form of humility we will ever know. It is evidence of a great faith in one's own ground, one's own star, a religious faith, perhaps, that cannot be broken down, and we should not call it arrogance."[9]

He expressed something similar when he said, "Your soul is the real you. The soul is the essence of you, the essential you. Your spirit is the temper, color, and expressiveness of your soul."[10]

On a more personal note, he also remarked:

"If you were to deduct Froebel, Goethe, Beethoven, and Nietzsche from my education I should be very much the poorer."[11]

"Of all the fine arts, music it was that I could not live without—as taught by my father (the symphony an edifice of sound). [I] found in it [a] sympathetic parallel to architecture.

Beethoven, and Bach too, were princely architects in my spiritual realm."[12]

In these excerpts from the Sunday morning talks a strong sense of ethics prevailed, and Wright clearly stated the difference between ethics and morals: "Morals are the customs which are conceded to be, or considered to be, the good ones as against the bad ones. When we say a moral man we mean a man who, according to the tenor and judgment of his time, does the right thing. But it may not be, in any ethical analysis, the true thing. When you speak of ethics, then you are getting to the actual organic nature of right and wrong. Ethics and morality have very little in common."[13] Giving a specific example, Wright pointed out that "the truly ethical person would be more in a fix than Jesus himself was. He was truly ethical. You could not speak of Jesus as a moral man. That would be degrading. It would make him of his time and of his day, which, of course, he was not."[14]

Although he deplored organized Christian religion, believing that it did not fully reflect the teachings of Jesus, Wright was basically a deeply religious person.

11

"The great thing for us is faith—faith in the incarnation—faith in its quality, in its inevitability, in its indestructibility. That is what we call religion—should call religion. And that religion is the greatest religion which gives you most strength and courage in that faith."[15]

"There is nothing higher, that I can see, than the deep and full understanding and appreciation of the beauty around you—the beauty of the idea we call Nature, the body you might say, who made the body of God the Great Idea."[16]

Bruce Brooks Pfeiffer
Director
Frank Lloyd Wright Archives

NOTES

1. Frank Lloyd Wright, "Recollections—United States, 1893–1920," *Architects Journal of London,* August 6, 1936, 174.

2. Frank Lloyd Wright, *An Organic Architecture,* in *Collected Writings, Volume 3, 1931–1933,* ed. Bruce Brooks Pfeiffer (New York: Rizzoli, 1993), 331.

3. *Frank Lloyd Wright: His Living Voice,* selected and with commentary by Bruce Brooks Pfeiffer (Fresno: Press at California State University, Fresno, 1987), 206.

4. Baker Brownell and Frank Lloyd Wright, *Architecture and Modern Life* (New York: Harper, 1937), 19–20.

5. Transcript of tape recordings made of Frank Lloyd Wright speaking between 1949 and 1959, Frank Lloyd Wright Foundation Archives, Taliesin West, Scottsdale, Arizona, no. 145, 1. (Hereafter this source is abbreviated as "TT.")

6. TT no. 95, 1.

7. TT no. 29, 1.

8. TT no. 241, 12.

9. TT no. 286, 8.

10. TT no. 47, 20.

11. TT no. 129, 12.

12. Frank Lloyd Wright, *A Testament* (New York: Horizon, 1957), 206.

13. TT no. 46, 8.

14. Ibid., 8–9.

15. TT no. 47, 23.

16. TT no. 214, 1.

ARCHITECTURE

DEFINITIONS

Architecture is the triumph of human imagination over materials, methods, and men to put man into possession of his own earth. *1930*

What does the word *architect* mean? The exact translation would be *the master of the know-how*. *Arch*—high, like archbishop, arch-this, arch-that. *Tect*—meaning technique, know-how. So you get *architect*—master of the know-how. *1954*

> *There is no architecture without a philosophy.*
> *There is no art of any kind without its own*
> *philosophy.* 1959

All the color and texture the eye has seen—all the rhythms the ear has heard—all the grace of form the mind may grasp—are properties of architecture. *1931*

Architecture is the scientific art of making structure express ideas. *1930*

The mission of an architect is to help people understand how to make life more beautiful, the world a better one for living in, and to give reason, rhyme, and meaning to life. *1957*

We have great bridges all over the world. A great bridge may be great architecture in the true sense, but the more they are let alone by architects the more they are great bridges. *1932*

WHAT IS NEEDED MORE IN ARCHITECTURE—JUST WHAT IT IS IN HUMAN LIFE—INTEGRITY. *1954*

Whenever architecture was great it was modern, and whenever architecture was modern human values were the only values preserved. *1931*

I know that architecture is life; or at least it is life itself taking form and therefore is the truest record of life as it was lived in the world yesterday, as it is being lived today or ever will be lived. *1939*

Architecture is the frame of life. It is the nature and substance of whatever is. *1955*

BUILDING IN NATURE

I began to see a building primarily not as a cave but as broad shelter in the open, related to vista; vista without and vista within. *1954*

Man takes a positive hand in creation whenever he puts a building upon the earth beneath the sun. If he has birthright at all, it must consist in this: that he, too, is no less a feature of the landscape than the rocks, trees, bears or bees of that nature to which he owes his being. *1937*

The good building is not one that hurts the landscape, but is one that makes the landscape more beautiful than it was before that building was built. *1957*

> *A house, we like to believe, is* in status quo *a noble consort to man and the trees; therefore the house should have repose and such texture as will quiet the whole and make it graciously at one with external nature.* 1931

Of the ground and into the light is the first basis of a good house. Looking at it, you could not imagine it anywhere but right there. *1955*

ORGANIC ARCHITECTURE

By organic architecture I mean an architecture that *develops* from within outward in harmony with the conditions of its being, as distinguished from one that is *applied* from without. *1914*

This gospel of organic architecture still has more in sympathy and in common with Oriental thought than it has with any other thing the West has confessed . . . It cannot truthfully be said, however, that organic architecture was derived from the Orient. We have our own way of putting these elemental (so ancient) ideals into practical effect . . . The idea of organic architecture that the reality of the building lies in the space within to be lived in, the feeling that we must not enclose ourselves in an envelope which is the building, is not alone Oriental. Democracy, proclaiming the integrity of the individual *per se*, had the feeling if not the words. *1954*

The proposed new building for the Guggenheim Museum . . . is the latest sense of organic architecture. Here we are not building a cellular composition of compartments, but one where all is one great space on a single continuous floor. The eye encounters no abrupt change, but is gently led and treated as if at the edge of the shore watching an unbreaking wave. *1953*

> ORGANIC ARCHITECTURE IS . . . ARCHITEC-
> TURE IN THE REFLEX, ARCHITECTURE SEEKING
> TO SERVE MAN RATHER THAN TO BECOME,
> OR BE BECOMING TO, ONE OF THOSE FORCES
> THAT TRY SO HARD TO RULE OVER HIM. *1945*

Organic architecture is American architecture; it is America's contribution to the architecture of the world. Not the International style, not any style at all, but an enlightenment. Not a conditioning of the mind, not a conditioning of the soul, but an enlight-enment of the mind concerning these things which are fundamental to a culture of our own. *1954*

20

ARCHITECTURE AS CULTURE

Architecture is that great living creative spirit which from generation to generation, from age to age, proceeds, persists, creates, according to the nature of man, and his circumstances as they both *change*. That really is architecture. *1939*

There is no such thing as an architect who is but one thing, or limited in his views, in his outlook. He must be the most comprehensive of all the masters, the most comprehensive of all the human beings on earth. His work is the thing that is entrusted to him by way of his virtue, is most broad of all. *1954*

If there is architecture in Mars or Venus, and there is, at least there is the architecture of Mars and Venus themselves—the same principles are at work there, too. Principles are universal. *1931*

Never miss the idea that architecture and music belong together. They are practically one. *1957*

What I call integral ornament is founded upon the same organic simplicities as Beethoven's Fifth Symphony, that amazing revolution in tumult and splendor of sound built upon four tones, based upon a rhythm a child could play on the piano with one finger. Supreme imagination reared the four repeated tones, simple rhythms, into a great symphonic poem that is probably the noblest thought-built edifice in our world. And architecture is like music in this capacity for the symphony. *1955*

What a great thing it would have been for us if, on the *Mayflower*, there had been a genuine architect, a creative architect. *1958*

Architecture must now construct anew the whole social pattern of our time as a new order of the human spirit. *1936*

Architecture is basic to culture. Music is an attribute of culture, so is painting, so would sculpture be. But architecture you experience; the other things you accede to. So without architecture you cannot have a culture. *1952*

I believe architecture to be the *humanizing* of building. The more humane, the more rich and significant, inviting and charming your architecture becomes, the more truly it is the great basis of a true culture. *1949*

PRACTICAL ADVICE

The physician can bury his mistakes, but the architect can only advise his client to plant vines—so they should go as far as possible from home to build their first buildings. *1953*

The cardinal sin in architecture is overdoing anything. 1957

23

....

Rhythm in a building is largely a question of the third dimension or the depth of the building. A thing is out of place when it is not in rhythm. And what is rhythm in a building? In music you listen to it, in painting you look at it, in a building you live with it. *1952*

By way of innate sense of comfort, had come the idea that the size of the human figure should fix every proportion of a dwelling or of anything in it. Human scale was true building scale. *1954*

SENTIMENTALITY IS, OF COURSE, SENTIMENT GONE TO SEED. SENTIMENTALITY IS SOMETHING DEAD AND INEXPRESSIBLE. STAY AWAY FROM IT. *1952*

Decoration is intended to make use more charming and comfort more appropriate, or else a privilege has been abused. *1943*

A sense of proportion is a conscientious realization of limitation. *1958*

The traffic problem is the problem the architect must meet and solve first . . . Unless the motor car problem is first of all solved—approached and solved—I see no reason for building beautiful, expensive, monumental buildings. *1958*

ARCHITECT AS SEER

The architect must be the master in the interior sense, not only of his tools, not only of his materials, but also of the human spirit. The soul of humanity is in his charge, really. *1958*

In architecture, as in life, to separate spirit and matter is to destroy both. *1937*

When Jesus said "The Kingdom of God is within you"—within *you* there is the basis of organic thought, in architecture, too. The reality of the thing is the within, and it is within, and it radiates, and you feel it, and if you feel it strong enough, you can build it. *1955*

Architecture is a great spirit that has pervaded the world ever since man began to make marks on the wall of his cave and tried to make what he lived in consonant with his environment and beautiful. Savages seem to have made a better job of it than civilized people. *1955*

The complete architect . . . is master of the elements: earth, air, fire, light, and water. Space, motion, and gravitation are his palette: the sun his brush. His concern is the heart of humanity. He, of all men, must see into the life of things; know their honor. *1949*

REACTIONS

Poetic tranquility instead of a more deadly "efficiency," should be the consequence in the art of building: concordant, sane, exuberant, and appropriate to purpose. Durable, serviceable, economical. Beautiful. *1957*

Everybody goes to the Capitol in Washington and is impressed. Of course that is what the Capitol was built to do—to give humanity an inferiority complex. *1957*

I remember how as a boy, primitive American architecture—Toltec, Aztec, Mayan, Inca—stirred my wonder, excited my wishful admiration. I wished I might someday have money enough to go to Mexico, Guatemala and Peru to join in excavating those long slumbering remains of lost cultures; mighty, primitive abstractions of man's culture—ancient arts of the Mayan, the Inca, the Toltec . . . A grandeur arose in the scale of total building never since excelled, seldom equalled by man either in truth of plan or simple primitive integrity of form. Architecture intrinsic to time, place and man. *1957*

27

NATURE

In nature there is a continuous, ceaseless becoming. There is the great in-between of which Lao-tze speaks, which is alive, which never ceases to be. *1954*

Organic simplicity might be seen producing significant character in the harmonious order we call Nature: all around, beauty in growing things. None insignificant. *1931*

Simplicity is a clean, direct expression of that thing which is itself. A wildflower has simplicity; a cultivated flower seldom has. Cultivation seems to go against that simplicity in the flower, and it does the same thing in human life. *1954*

NATURE IS YOUR BOOK OF REFERENCE, AND IN IT YOU STUDY AND LEARN. *1955*

Frederick Froebel, the founder of the kindergarten, declared you should not just go out and look at nature and draw these natural effects, but you should go *into* nature—find out the forms that are elemental. *1955*

A flower is an intangible. It may be an eye looking out on us from the great inner sea of beauty and precious beyond words. *1954*

The [Welsh] definition of genius was very simple, very true, and very good: A man who can see nature; a man who has a heart for nature (that is, who loves nature), and a man who had the courage to follow nature. *1956*

Everything that is romantic is of nature. *1957*

Go outdoors and look at the trees. See the specimens of foliage and new ones springing up all the while. Go in a garden and watch the flowers. It is just one principle—the principle is the same in every one, but see the enormous variety. *1948*

[If] you form the habit of nature study, little by little you will find your faculties strengthened, refreshed, and capable of more effective interpenetration, and it will go on as long as you will. *1957*

That which is according to nature survives. That which is contrary to nature disappears. As it is true to nature, there is where you place your platform, where you can put your feet, and stand there and never be deceived. *1959*

Art is a discovery and development of elementary principles of nature into beautiful forms suitable for human use. 1957

My mother used to cut flowers with great long stems and put them in glass [vases] always so she could see the stems in the water, and I have inherited that—I like to see that, too. *1957*

When I say *nature* I do not mean the wind and the bees and the trees and the animals. I mean the nature with a capital "N" that is the essence of life everywhere, the essence of life itself. *1959*

You might say that nature is the God of the architect. *1953*

THE SOUL + FAITH

I do not believe you can build beautiful buildings, that true edifices can arise, except that they come from a worthy source, and that source is inevitably the human soul, the human heart. *1950*

This age we are living in is going to be known as the "Sanitary Age," the age in which we have bathtubs, water closets, and running water—and no soul. *1951*

"BE CLEAN!" "BE CLEAN" WAS THE SOUL OF SHINTO . . . SHINTO SPOKE NOT OF A GOOD MAN, NOR SPOKE OF A MORAL MAN, BUT SPOKE OF A CLEAN MAN. SHINTO SPOKE NOT ONLY OF CLEAN HANDS, BUT OF A CLEAN HEART. *1931*

The recuperative power of the human frame, human body, if coupled with the right kind of spirit, is almost invincible. *1957*

Your strength physically is nothing without the spiritual strength that should go with it. *1958*

Respect the masterpiece—it is true reverence to man. There is no quality so great, none so much needed now. *1931*

Good reading of the great poets is just as essential to the spiritual life as sitting down at the table and eating when you are hungry. *1955*

Integrity is the first law of the spirit. *1956*

I am inclined to think that the time scale is a very serious impediment to the development of the interior quality of the human soul. *1952*

There is a deadly tendency toward conformity which in the human spirit is something like gangrene in the human flesh. *1958*

I think that nothing can improve except as the soul improves, and if the soul improves the spirit radiates it immediately, because spirit radiates the soul. *1952*

Your soul is you and that soul produces what is called your spirit . . . The soul is the essence of you, the essential you. Your spirit is the temper, color, and expressiveness of your soul. *1952*

The main thing is to keep an open mind and a contributing spirit, not get stiffened and shutting things out, but receptive, willing, and eager to get hold of what is true against what is false. And that is the best road forward. *1959*

To have a cause and a loyalty at heart for a cause that is deep and profound will give your manhood a fine stance. You will be square on your spiritual feet. *1958*

Lao-tze declared that as soon as anything became tangible, it was dead. It is only the intangibles that are living and have the power of becoming. *1957*

I have an ideal and that ideal is all I ever expect to see of God, and I believe in my ideal so I believe in God. *1952*

I believe that incarnation is always and forever in some form or other. I do not think that we ever lose that incarnation. Now what forms it may take in afterlife, how that incarnation is to keep manifesting itself through the various changes of time in the universe, I do not know and I do not think anyone knows. *1952*

> *The great thing for us is faith—faith in the incarnation—faith in its quality, in its inevitability, in its indestructibility. That is what we call religion—should call religion. And that religion is the greatest religion, which gives you most strength and courage in that faith.* 1952

Really to believe in something is the greatest boon, I think, and to believe wholeheartedly in it and to serve it with all your strength and your might is salvation. *1958*

A man's conscience is really the mainspring of what he, with some reason, might call his soul. So listen attentively to conscience, always. *1958*

I have talked of honest arrogance, but there is no such thing as honest arrogance. Arrogance is only arrogance when it has nothing under it, when it has nothing to stand on, when it is a pretense, a quackery, or a fake. When it is genuine it is a pride that is the highest form of humility we will ever know. It is evidence of a great faith in one's own ground, one's own star, a religious faith, perhaps, and that cannot be broken down and we should not call it arrogance. *1953*

Einstein was the greatest of the scientists. He was the man who confessed that science would find— after all was done, all calculations on record, all achievements—that it was up to the final reality, and that reality was art and religion. *1959*

I don't see any reason why anyone should ever age; they can grow old in years; their faculties can diminish physically. But as they diminish physically, they should increase spiritually. And there is a compensation there that should make elderly people, people of experience, more and more valuable as they grow older, instead of less and less so. *1950*

Insofar as I am immortal, I will be immortal. 1957

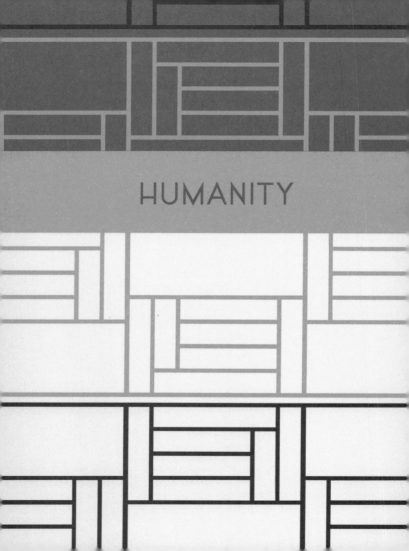

HUMANITY

Youth is a quality once you achieve you never lose it, and I guess if you die with it, you are immortal. *1954*

The greatest harm that man can do in life is to spoil the faith, the trust, and the fresh vision of the child. 1956

We hunger for POETRY naturally as we do for sunlight, fresh air, and fruits, if we are normal human beings. *1928*

What really does humanity want? Of course we know the answer: three squares a day, fornication, and a good snore. And above that, not much else. *1951*

The great man is the man who deals in realities as the intangibles of today. *1954*

If you are going to remain free, you must be free by way of your conscience and your ability to think. *1957*

Arrogance is something a man possesses on the surface to defend the fact that he hasn't got the things he pretends to have. He's a bluff, in other words. *1957*

Sentiment is an honorable, desirous state. Now when you become sentimental, then that is the good thing gone over the board, gone wrong, and where an excess ruins its integrity and its beauty. *1954*

The one great truth of which mankind could be certain: that all was to change; that all was in a process of change; and the law of change was the valid, visible law which man could comprehend. *1954*

I DO NOT THINK WE SHOULD BE TOO CONTENT, TOO SATISFIED, WITH ANYTHING, AT ANY TIME, WHATSOEVER. *1957*

I think hardship is necessarily invaluable. Without it there could be no growth, and I think that suffering is absolutely essential to growth. *1957*

*Humanity cannot exist without a love of and a
sense of and a desire for the superior thing.* 1955

The uncommon man is the man who can fall in love
with an idea, the man who can subscribe to an idea
and who realizes the nature of an idea. *1958*

Ridicule is just that of the buffoon. Ridicule is
something on the surface and much easier to
practice and what you usually get in the name
of humor. *1953*

Humor is pathos, never far from tears. You can laugh
and cry when you laugh. *1958*

You can only become extrovert as you have been
introvert, that is, as you have been perceptive, as you
have perceived, taken into yourself, something you
can give. *1948*

No man climbs so high or sinks so low that he isn't eager to receive the good will and admiration of his fellow men . . . He may hitch his wagon to his star, but however he may be circumstanced or whatever his ideals or his actions, he never loses desire for the approbation of his kind. *1949*

HUMAN NATURE IS SO CONSTRUCTED THAT IT HAS AN INNATE SYMPATHY WITH THOSE THINGS WITH WHICH IT HAS ASSOCIATED JOY, DIGNITY, AND GOOD LUCK. *1948*

Humor has in it something close to tears; it goes deep into human nature. *1953*

It is only as the squeeze comes on that the truth comes out; and so, with adversity as the hammer, I guess, the forge in which the character is made. *1954*

I do think that a sense of humor is one of the most valuable things you can possess. 1958

When the struggle ends, and when there is no longer a demand upon your faculties to surmount, to achieve, and to become, you are dead. *1954*

WISDOM

I lived with all the expressions of beauty I could see. And all those that I could acquire and use for study and enjoyment I acquired as my library, but living with them all as I might. *1957*

A man is wise from within . . . and from that within comes this mystical quality of the human soul which we call wisdom. *1954*

THE FRESH MIND SEES WITH A SEEING EYE AND IS LIKELY TO SEE TRUTH. BUT THE MORE YOU ARE EDUCATED AND THE MORE YOU ARE CONDITIONED, THE LESS ABLE YOU BECOME TO SEE STRAIGHT. *1956*

Honor your father and mother always, and don't believe what you read in the newspapers. *1954*

→ Letter to Janice Kimberlin, 6th grade

A matter of taste is usually a matter of ignorance. *1931*

47

Education, of course, is always based upon what *was*. Education shows you what has been and leaves you to make the deduction as to what may be. Education as we pursue it cannot prophesy, and does not. *1955*

One should never dwell on one's failures. You should think about them only enough to gain the wisdom from them that they will afford. *1956*

True education in architecture, in anything else, would consist in the ability to respond to and appreciate the beautiful, and to consider it as the highest and the finest kind of morality. *1955*

AN EXPERT IS A MAN WHO HAS STOPPED THINKING BECAUSE "HE KNOWS." *1957*

Publicity seems to be the blood circulating in the intellectual veins of the nation. *1957*

Wisdom in the human-bud becomes fragrance in the human flower. 1959

I think the only basis for criticism is love, a feeling of love for the thing that you are talking about and you are expressing. Only as you *understand* that thing have you any right to criticize. *1954*

Emerson today is the strongest, purest, finest mind this country has ever produced, and everybody should read him daily. *1951*

Love is only a kind of understanding. What you understand is the extent and the measure of your power to love anything. *1950*

A great architect is not made by way of a brain nearly so much as by way of a cultivated, enriched heart. It is the love of the thing that he does that really qualifies him in the end. *1952*

The inferior mind always tries to learn by comparison, but the deeper mind, the good mind, learns by analysis. *1956*

The present system of education is the trampling of the herd. *1956*

Fear is usually coupled, and inevitably is, with ignorance. 1952

If you have actual knowledge concerning certain truths in relation to building or painting or music or sculpture, those are the things that will grow and endure and eventually persist. *1959*

True study is a form of experience. *1958*

Cultivate the poet. The poet is the unacknowledged legislator of this universe and the sooner we knock under to that the better. Get Emerson's essay on the American scholar and read it once a year. *1957*

If you are going to read, you should read something
that will feed you, build you up, strengthen you and
be what you need to know. *1957*

Never have I thought of an educated man as a cultured
man, a cultured human being. *1958*

Culture is developed from within and education is
to be groomed from without. *1959*

The old academic order is bulging with its own
important impotence. *1954*

A MARITAL BUREAU AND A TRADE SCHOOL IS
WHAT THE UNIVERSITIES, SO CALLED, HAVE
DEGENERATED TO IN OUR COUNTRY. *1948*

When anyone becomes an authority, that is the end
of him so far as development is concerned. *1948*

51

CREATIVITY

An idea is salvation by imagination. *1931*

There is nothing so inspiring to the spirit of a boy who wants to design something as a beautiful stretch, a blank sheet of paper, T square, triangle, and a pencil. *1958*

May your own genius inspire and keep you as a blessing to your time and place. *1956*
> *Letter to former apprentice Andrew Devane*

> *Creation is something within, the nature of an experience moving outward into life with great consequences.* 1951

When you become the pencil in the hand of the infinite, when you are truly creative in your attempt to design, the thing that we call good design begins and never has an end. Once you are aware of the importance of this spirit living in nature, you will never have to copy nature. *1954*

I think the worst thing that can happen is to publish your work prematurely. *1950*

It is those little *things that you do and that you do with your feeling and with your heart that are really constructive.* 1954

Invention is not creation. To invent something is not creative. *1952*

This design matter is not something to do with a drawing board. It is something you do as you work, as you play. You may get it in the middle of the tennis court, and drop your racket, run off, and put it down. That is the kind of thing that it is. It is fleeting; it is evanescent. *1954*

Vision has to have some guidance and motivation or it will simply see things as they are, not as they ought to be. *1955*

To be creative as an individual you must be in yourselves qualified. And to be qualified, you must have quality. *1952*

It is imitation of imitation that destroys an original tradition. To be loyal to tradition, you have to understand it as a great central motivating factor. *1953*

Too much success, too much ease, too much food, too much of anything, is the end of the creative endeavor. *1954*

THERE IS NO SUCH THING AS AN ARTIST WITHOUT A PHILOSOPHY. *1952*

The song, the masterpiece, the edifice are a warm out-pouring of the heart of man—human delight in life triumphant: we glimpse the infinite. *1931*

There is no artist without his religion, without his philosophy, without his faith in mankind. *1958*

I do not think you are a real photographer until you develop your own plates, because in the development comes a great deal of the effect. *1959*

I HAVE NEVER WANTED TO BE FINISHED.
I HAVE NEVER WANTED TO FEEL THAT WHAT I
HAVE DONE WAS THE BEST I COULD DO . . .
I HAVE TO BE CAREFUL OF THAT BECAUSE
THAT IS POISON TO THE CREATIVE SPIRIT. *1952*

Creative instinct belongs to the human race. It has manifested itself in so many different ways down the ages—Oriental, Western, modern, southern, northern. It has all come from the same source, the same stream. And that source is not the brain, it is not the head, it is not the intellect—it is the heart. It is the warmth of heart and the love of life, that really is the best mainspring for an artist creating anything, no matter what it is. *c. 1957*

The moment a thing becomes a fixed point, it is dead. The true living thing is always in between and in a state of becoming. *1957*

BEAUTY

I BELIEVE A HOUSE IS MORE A HOME
BY BEING A WORK OF ART. *1954*

As beautiful building after beautiful building gets itself
constructed and built, they will begin to look into it
and try to find out what the secret was that kept it
perennially young and always working and never let it
die because it couldn't die. A principle never dies. *1952*

Could you imagine anything more dreary than modern
civilization without anything of beauty in it at all? Just
what they call practical. I cannot think of anything
more dead, more stupid, more of a thing I'd like to get
away from. *1952*

The thing that is lost to us most completely now, I
think, is the capacity to draw the line between what
is merely curious and what is really beautiful. *1951*

What is good in our present civilization is still a
hankering after something beautiful. *1955*

Color has a significance all its own, and is in a realm all its own. Color is the music of light, you see. *1953*

A civilization can occur by way of science, and science can maintain a civilization up to a certain point. But culture is a way of making that way of life which is a civilization beautiful. *1952*

I believe that Emerson was right when he said, "Beauty is the highest and finest kind of morality." If you are attuned—and you love sincerely—harmony, rhythm, and what we call beauty, instinctively what is ugly will become offensive to you. It will come into the realm of the spirit also. You will see how certain actions of your own are ugly, how certain of others are beautiful. *1955*

A man without a sense of beauty is like a ship without a rudder: no place to go but out and no place to come but back. *1955*

Instinctively and naturally, if you beautify your own life, you beautify the life of everybody around you. *1956*

It is the *quality* in things that should make them desirable and beautiful, the joy forever that is ever and will always be the most important thing to mankind. *1949*

COLORS—IN PASTE OR CRAYON—OR PENCILS —ALWAYS A THRILL! TO THIS DAY I LOVE TO HOLD A HANDFUL OF MANY-COLORED PENCILS AND OPEN MY HAND TO SEE THEM LYING LOOSE UPON MY PALM, IN THE LIGHT. *1928*

We are all here to develop a life more beautiful, more concordant, more fully expressive of our own sense of pride and joy than ever before in the world. *1957*

To make anything beautiful is to make it naturally lovable, for it to have charm, for it to be genuine, for it to be an expression of all that is worth having or worth living for in our universe today. *1957*

When you have the sense of the whole, as harmonious, then you begin to express what we call the beautiful and you yourselves become artists. *1957*

IF YOU WANT A FRIEND AND COUNSELOR AND GUIDE, THERE IS ONE, AND THAT LIES IN THE HEART, NOT SO MUCH IN THE HEAD. IT IS THE LOVE OF BEAUTY, THE DESIRE IN YOUR HEART TO LEAVE THIS PLACE INTO WHICH YOU WERE BORN A BETTER PLACE TO LIVE IN BECAUSE YOU LIVED THERE, AND BECAUSE YOU HAVE LIVED AS YOU HAVE LIVED. *1954*

Nothing is worth a man's time—and that means a woman's—except a search for the beautiful, and an attempt to establish it in human life by way of the human being and his existence. *1952*

When you are on the track of an origin, which is a wonderful track to pursue, you will get back to the fact that the earlier the thing occurred, in the first simplicity of the burst forth of the idea, that was when it was most effective, most beautiful. *1958*

The element of color—it is another world. That probably is the most mysterious world of all— even more mysterious than form. 1952

CULTURE + VALUES

A CULTURE IS THE JOY OF LIVING, AND THE BEAUTY OF LIVING. *1951*

I never like to think back to Rome, because Rome was already degenerate, and I think Rome in its day was where we are in our day. *1950*

A civilization is just a way of life, and there have been hundreds of them, thousands of them in the world. But a culture is the way of making that life beautiful. *1953*

Culture has always been an import. Very seldom has culture ever sprung from the ground by way of a native. *1951*

Conscience is really the soul of freedom. 1953

I firmly believe that if you give the right thing to people to see and really experience, they will choose the right thing. *1955*

The artist himself, of course, is of his time, or he is not an artist. He is the prophet of his time and of his day; he is the seeing-eye of his people. He can see a little further and more clearly than his people see. That is why he is an artist. That is why the prophetic poet is the greatest of all the members of his civilization. *1955*

Culture means taking the thing according to its nature, giving it freedom, and the thing that it loves most and best and encouraging it to grow, and giving it materials to grow with. *1956*

The world had never had a culture until it had an architecture. The architecture was the basis of its culture, rather than the culture the basis of its architecture. *1958*

In any final result there can be no separation between our architecture and our culture. Nor any separation of either from our happiness. Nor any separation from our work. *1954*

I respect any man or woman who respects himself sufficiently to tell the truth no matter what or who it might hurt. *1957*

The growth of your souls, the expression of that thing that is you, is a matter of culture. *1959*

Quality consists in a developed consciousness and in a capacity for complete correlation of your faculties. If you are not a correlated human being, you are fragmentary, you are awkward, you are not there in any sense with the thing that is needed to be there. *1952*

QUALITY AND QUANTITY ARE NOT ON SPEAKING TERMS—NEVER CAN BE. *1956*

Your conscience is your guiding star and the finest thing about you in principle where manhood or womanhood is concerned. *1958*

Principles are always major. Ways and means are always minor, and they will arrange themselves in relation to the center line of principle. *1952*

Conscience and freedom are inalienable companions. 1956

Morals are the customs which are conceded to be, or considered to be, at that time, the good ones as against the bad ones. When we say a moral man we mean a man who, according to the tenor and judgment of his time, does the right thing. But it may not be, in any ethical analysis, the true thing. *1952*

THE WORKING OF A PRINCIPLE IS THE ONLY SAFE TRADITION. *1931*

The prefabricated house is inevitable, and a good thing. *1958*

When you speak of ethics, then you are getting to the actual organic nature of right and wrong. Ethics and morality have very little in common. *1952*

It is so easy when you know a principle to allow that principle to work for you and to do astonishingly sound and beautiful new expressions. Because there is no end to that. *1953*

There is no substitute for intrinsic responsibility, innate responsibility for your own acts, for your own character, and for your own self. *1957*

The best denial is the right affirmation. *1957*

DEMOCRACY + THE INDIVIDUAL

There is no such thing as creative except by the individual. Humanity, especially on a democratic basis, lives only by virtue of individuality. *1954*

I believe the man is more a man by being an individual rather than a committee-meeting. *1954*

Conformity is the death of the thing nature would call life. *1957*

I do not believe in force, and I do not believe in ganging up on anything. I believe in individuality and the power and effect of the individual's convictions and contributions. *1956*

DEMOCRACY CAN LIVE BY GENIUS ONLY. ITS VERY SOUL IS INDIVIDUALITY. *1918*

Everyone professing democracy should have not only an open mind but a certain charity of the soul that appreciates the qualities in others. *1952*

We are beginning to learn that the highest and finest kind of morality is beauty, and that there is no culture for democracy until it has one of its own. *1951*

Nature is manifestly in love with what we call individuality. Individuality is something precious in this world to be preserved, and I would hate to see any of it sacrificed in some foolish endeavor in the direction of "internationalism." 1948

Paradise for me would be a democracy where the poetic principle was inviolate and . . . the basis of all judgments. The new integrity. *1957*

GOVERNMENT

I think that government is totally unqualified to take a hand in culture. Culture, so far as government is concerned, never was a matter that would be legitimate in its hands. *1954*

FEAR IS THE ELEMENT THROUGH WHICH WE ARE GOVERNED, AND THAT IS WHY WE HAVE GOVERNMENT TODAY—BECAUSE FEAR IS EFFECTIVE. *1955*

I think one war only breeds another, and I have been borne out by a reading of history. One war always has in its intestines another, and another has another. *1957*

If we were all aware of the principle of humanity by which we live, war would have no being—there would be no war. If statesmanship truly represented the sentiment of the people themselves, there would be no war. *1957*

To place too great an emphasis on the common man is to glorify mediocrity. *1956*

HUMANITY, TO ME, IS NOT A MOB. THE MOB IS THE DEGENERATION OF HUMANITY; THE MOB IS HUMANITY GOING THE WRONG WAY. *1957*

It is notorious that the human animal is of such a character and nature that he cannot be trusted with authority. And just when we need quality the most, here comes mediocrity rising into high places. We have the domination of the mediocre. *1957*

WORK + SUCCESS

What a man does—*that* he has. You may find other things on him but they are not his. *1954*

There is no real development without integrity, that is—a love of truth. *1957*

I consider myself a success only insofar as my life is useful, revealing, and rewarding to my kind. *1957*

Principles are limitations because in the principle lies direction. Principles are hard masters, and you need to know that in order to do great work, work that will stand. *1952*

I BELIEVE THAT IN THE SEARCH FOR THE ANSWER LIES THE ANSWER. *1950*

If you have not had experience in connection with the thing that you are doing, you are going to make a fool of yourself or somebody else. Probably all together. *1953*

I am sure if I had not elected to live with my work, I never could have done even half what I have accomplished. I think that is the secret of really being productive, is to stay with it. *1958*

I do not believe you know what fun is until you know what hard work is. I think that out of that reflex from hard work comes real fun, comes real enjoyment of the things that are more excellent, the things that are poetry and the things that are music and the things that are beauty. 1958

You have to go wholeheartedly into anything in order to achieve anything worth having. *1958*

You do not learn by way of your successes. No one does. Your successes gradually build a wall between you and your creative self. You cannot afford to let that happen. You must always keep that wall aside so that you can see out. *1952*

According to our strength of character and our clarity of vision, we will endure, we will succeed, we will have contributed something to make life where we were and as we lived it, something a little better, brighter, and more beautiful. *1954*

WRIGHT ON WRIGHT

I never had the courage to lie. *1957*

My father was a preacher and musician. He taught me to regard a symphony as an edifice of sound. And ever since I have been listening to the great orchestras of the world as I would look at a building. *1951*

If you were to deduct Froebel*, Goethe, Beethoven, and Nietzsche from my education, I should be very much the poorer. *1955*

I wanted to be developed into an individual capable of honoring the profession I was in, not selling it down the river. *1951*

Japanese prints as I first saw them changed my way of looking at nature. *1952*

---

* Friedrich Froebel (1782–1852) was a German educational innovator whose ideas influenced Frank Lloyd Wright's mother, Anna Lloyd Jones Wright.

I know in my own case that nothing has been of any great value or lasting benefit to me or anybody else except as I have put my feet down where I could do something to make the world a little more beautiful. *1952*

I never sit down to a drawing board—and this has been a lifelong practice of mine—until I have the whole thing in my mind. I may alter it substantially, I may throw it away, I may find I'm up a blind alley, but unless I have the idea pretty well in shape, you won't see me at the drawing board with it. *1954*

I had to choose early in my life between an honest arrogance and a hypocritical humility, and I deliberately chose an honest arrogance. 1952

I have never had any greater pleasure than to take a handful of colored pencils in one hand here, T square and triangle lying on a sheet of white paper, and try to feel the design of the thing I want to do. It's a great moment. *1953*

I BELIEVE MYSELF THAT I HAVE LEARNED
FROM MY MISTAKES THE MOST. YOU WILL
NEVER LEARN ANYTHING FROM YOUR
SUCCESSES. *1951*

To cut ambiguity short: there never was exterior influence upon my work, either foreign or native, other than that of Lieber Meister*, Dankmar Adler and John Roebling, Whitman and Emerson, and the great poets worldwide. My work is original not only in fact but in spiritual fiber. No practice by any European architect to this day has influenced mine in the least. *1957*

I have been practicing architecture some sixty-one years, and I can still feel that all I need is another chance to do a good building. The next one will be it. *1952*

---

* The man whom Wright called Lieber Meister ("beloved master") was Louis Sullivan (1856–1924), a celebrated architect for whom Wright worked as a draftsman.

....

I have never in my life gone to anybody for a job. I have never turned my hand that much to ask a friend to say a word for me for a job, and yet I survive. *1958*

I have been black and blue in some spot, somewhere, almost all my life from too intimate contact with my own early furniture. *1954*

> I AM NOT A "MASTERPIECE MAN"—THE
> NEXT ONE I AM GOING TO DO IS ALWAYS
> THE BEST. WHEN A MAN POINTS TO HIS
> MASTERPIECE, HE IS FINISHED. DO NOT
> LOOK FOR MUCH FROM HIM. *c. 1957*

Romance is the flowering of the spirit, the flowering of the soul of man. It is of the man, of the circumstance, of the nature and the character of whatever he is himself . . . I have always confessed and represented myself as a romantic architect because romance is organic. *1957*

QUOTATION SOURCES

(ALL WORKS BY FRANK LLOYD WRIGHT UNLESS OTHERWISE NOTED.)

AML = Brownell, Baker, and Frank Lloyd Wright. *Architecture and Modern Life.* New York: Harper, 1937.

AU = *An Autobiography.* Petaluma, CA: Pomegranate, 2005.

CD = *Frank Lloyd Wright: The Crowning Decade, 1949–1959.* Selected and with commentary by Bruce Brooks Pfeiffer. Fresno: Press at California State University, Fresno, 1989.

CW1 = *Collected Writings, Volume 1, 1894–1931.* Edited by Bruce Brooks Pfeiffer. New York: Rizzoli, 1992.

CW2 = *Collected Writings, Volume 2, 1930–1932.* Edited by Bruce Brooks Pfeiffer. New York: Rizzoli, 1992.

CW3 = *Collected Writings, Volume 3, 1931–1939.* Edited by Bruce Brooks Pfeiffer. New York: Rizzoli, 1993.

CW4 = *Collected Writings, Volume 4, 1939–1949.* Edited by Bruce Brooks Pfeiffer. New York: Rizzoli, 1994.

HLV = *Frank Lloyd Wright: His Living Voice.* Selected

and with commentary by Bruce Brooks Pfeiffer. Fresno:
Press at California State University, Fresno, 1987.

MA = *Modern Architecture, Being the Kahn Lectures for
1930.* Princeton Monographs in Art and Archaeology.
Princeton, NJ: Princeton University Press, 1931.

NH = *The Natural House.* New York: Horizon, 1954.

TE = *A Testament.* New York: Horizon, 1957.

TL = *Two Lectures on Architecture.* Chicago: Art Intitute
of Chicago, 1931.

TT = Transcript of tape recordings made of Frank Lloyd
Wright speaking between 1949 and 1959. Frank Lloyd
Wright Foundation Archives, Taliesin West, Scottsdale,
Arizona.

WD = *When Democracy Builds.* Chicago: University of
Chicago Press, 1945.

ARCHITECTURE: *Definitions:* CW1, 340; TT no.
95, 5–6; TT no. 235, 21; MA, endpaper; CW1, 340;
TT no. 251, 5; TT no. 270, 22; TT no. 96, 36; TL, 49;
CW3, 331; TT no. 280, 2. *Building in Nature:* NH, 16;
CW3, 223; Frank Lloyd Wright, *Marin County Civic
Center* (San Francisco: Royal Blueprint Company, 1957),
no page numbers; CW2, 51; TT no. 259, 3. *Organic
Architecture:* CW1, 127; NH, 218–219; Aline B. Louchheim,
"Frank Lloyd Wright Talks of His Art," *New York Times
Magazine,* October 4, 1953, 47; WD, 53; TT no. 258, 9.
Architecture as Culture: CW3, 331; TT no. 110, 16–17;
TL, 49; TT no. 277, 28; Elizabeth Gordon, "The Sym-
phonic Poem of a Great House," *House Beautiful,* No-
vember 1955, 272; TT no. 213, 8; Frank Lloyd Wright,
"Recollections—United States, 1893–1920," *Architects
Journal of London,* August 6, 1936, 174; TT no. 51, 11;
TT no. 267, 12–13. *Practical Advice:* Louchheim, "Frank
Lloyd Wright Talks of His Art," 47; TT no. 187, 1; TT
no. 44, 28; NH, 17; TT no. 242, 12; AU, 145; HLV, 205;
TT no. 291, 4. *Architect as Seer:* HLV, 206; AML, 45;
TT no. 144, 23; TT no. 142, 9; CW4, 382. *Reactions:*
TE, 223; TT no. 195, 8; TE, 111–112.

NATURE: HLV, 178; TL, 13; TT no. 96, 39; TT no. 125, 25; TT no. 129, 10; TT no. 105, 2; TT no. 173, 4; TT no. 192, 9; TT no. 282, 18; TT no. 192, 22; TT no. 230, 19; TT no. 192, 6; TT no. 203, 13; TT no. 231, 17; TT no. 60, 3.

THE SOUL + FAITH: TT no. 256, 5; TT no. 26, 27; MA, 33; TT no. 204, 5; ibid.; TL, 63; TT no. 146, 9; TT no. 158, 17; TT no. 55, 7; TT no. 242, 13; TT no. 47, 21; TT no. 47, 20; TT no. 232, 7; TT no. 225, 10; TT no. 199, 16; TT no. 58, 9; TT no. 47, 22; TT no. 47, 23; HLV, 203; TT no. 225, 5; TT no. 286, 8; TT no. 233, 4; TT no. 10, 4; TT no. 299 (Mike Wallace interview), 310.

HUMANITY: TT no. 104b, 2; TT no. 152, 9; CW1, 314; TT no. 20, 10; TT no. 105, 2; TT no. 200, 9; CD, 80; TT no. 110, 16; TT no. 114, 10; TT no. 186, 11; TT no. 180, 5; TT no. 144, 13; TT no. 217, 5; TT no. 91, 3; TT no. 215, 5; TT no. 281, 25; CW4, 325; TT no. 282, 21; TT no. 91, 3; TT no. 114, 8; TT no. 215, 6; TT no. 114, 9.

WISDOM: TE, 207; TT no. 110, 8–9; TT no. 152, 9;
Frank Lloyd Wright to Janice Kimberlin (a sixth-grader),
March 6, 1954, Frank Lloyd Wright Foundation Archives, Taliesin West, Scottsdale, Arizona; MA, endpaper; TT no. 125, 8; TT no. 173, 10–11; TT no. 134,
9; Frank Lloyd Wright to Ralph Nader, December 24,
1957, Frank Lloyd Wright Foundation Archives, Taliesin
West, Scottsdale, Arizona; TT no. 199, 6; CD, 90; TT
no. 133, 3; TT no. 23, 2; TT no. 4, 3; TT no. 46, 5; TT
no. 160, 19; TT no. 162, 10; TT no. 56, p. 12; TT no.
230, 19; TT no. 213, 11; TT no. 276a, 227; TT no. 299
(Mike Wallace interview), 309; TT no. 217, 5; TT no.
231, 9; NH, 32; TT no. 281, 20; TT no. 285, 6.

CREATIVITY: TL, 11; TT no. 204, 10; Frank Lloyd
Wright to former apprentice Andrew Devane, March 27,
1956, Frank Lloyd Wright Foundation Archives, Taliesin
West, Scottsdale, Arizona; TT no. 29, 2; HLV, 178; TT
no. 12, 3; TT no. 133, 11; TT no. 41, 15; TT no. 113,
11; TT no. 139, 7; TT no. 50, 14; TT no. 62, 6; TT no.
114, 9; TT no. 58, 25; TL, 59; TT no. 207, 13; TT no.
233, 10; TT no. 46, 7; TT no. 260, 5; TT no. 183, 14.

BEAUTY: NH, endpaper; TT no. 44, 5; HLV, 123; TT no. 15, 13; TT no. 125, 19; TT no. 261, 11; TT no. 46, 22; TT no. 121, 8–9; TT no. 139, 15; TT no. 158, 15; CW4, 334; CW1, 269; TT no. 183, 18; TT no. 198, 6; TT no. 203, 13; TT no. 258, 18; TT no. 241, 14; TT no. 228, 5; TT no. 45, 14.

CULTURE + VALUES: TT no. 26, 20; TT no. 12, 6–7; HLV, 105; TT no. 15, 4; TT no. 86, 9; TT no. 142, 14; TT no. 125, 7; TT no. 160, 4; TT no. 213, 7; NH, 51; CD, 81; TT no. 231, 9; TT no. 50, 15; TT no. 176, 11; TT no. 225, 5; TT no. 44, 34; TT no. 304, 10; TT no. 46, 8; MA, endpaper; TT no. 205, 3; TT no. 46, 9; TT no. 78, 10; TT no. 184, 12; TT no. 199, 14.

DEMOCRACY + THE INDIVIDUAL: TT no. 113, 7; NH, endpaper; TT no. 180, 20; TT no. 176, 20; CW1, 159; TT no. 50, 2; TT no. 297, 1; TT no. 282, 16; Frank Lloyd Wright to Lynn Farnol, July 12, 1957, Frank Lloyd Wright Foundation Archives, Taliesin West, Scottsdale, Arizona.

GOVERNMENT: TT no. 117, 15; TT no. 139, 17; TT no. 299 (Mike Wallace interview), 294; TT no. 181, 32; TT no. 155, 3; TT no. 299 (Mike Wallace interview), 307; TT no. 201, 11.

WORK + SUCCESS: NH, 24; TT no. 180, 20; CD, 48; TT no. 44, 32; TT no. 12, 9; TT no. 71, 7; TT no. 204, 7; TT no. 213, 12; TT no. 225, 2; TT no. 46, 7; TT no. 110, 11.

WRIGHT ON WRIGHT: TE, 207; TT no. 23, 3; TT no. 129, 12; TT no. 18, 25; TT no. 41, 17; TT no. 275, 13; TT no. 113, 10; TT no. 241, 12; TT no. 81, 15–16; TT no. 26, 14; TE, 205; TT no. 57, 28; TT no. 257, 14; NH, 43; TT no. 260, 11; TT no. 191, 6–7.